AND AFTER THAT NURSE?

26
40

And after that
NURSE?

〜〜〜〜〜〜〜〜〜〜〜

Hundreds of nursing 'howlers' taken from the actual examination papers of many great hospitals

04269
ROGER BROOK
did the compilation

JACQUELINE MORAN
did the drawings

SOUVENIR PRESS · LONDON
looked the other way and published

First published 1966 by Souvenir Press Ltd.,
95 Mortimer Street, London, W.1 and simultaneously
in Canada by The Ryerson Press Ltd Toronto 2B.

**Printed in Great Britain by
Billing & Sons Limited, Guildford and London**

A Word from the Compiler

The television camera brings the nurse before us in all her saintliness—gleaming white uniform, dangling watch and thermometer at the ready. We can all add our own touches to the picture, but basically nurses all over the world command, and richly deserve, our respect and admiration.

Not the least of their virtues is a sense of humour. So I have no hesitation in presenting a third collection of howlers taken from nurses' examination papers. Under exam fever we can all make silly mistakes and it is very much to the credit of this fine profession that nurses, sisters and matrons have pounced on these books, read them with gales of laughter tinged with sympathy, and bought them in thousands to send to their friends and colleagues.

As a doctor responsible for marking examination papers I know that these howlers are not to be taken too seriously. Indeed our nurses need to laugh at themselves and their job in order to cope with the unpleasant drudgery which comes before the joy of seeing a patient go home well and happy.

Contents

Eat, Drink and Be Merry

For a test meal 2 tablespoonfuls of wheat are added to 1 quart of water and this is given to the patient after his stomach has been withdrawn with a syringe.

Males eaten hurriedly are probably the cause of peptic ulceration.

The patient said he knew he had indigestion badly because his heart was burning.

A high fitty diet is thought likely to cause coronary thrombosis.

The overweight patient was put on a very strict low silt diet.

After the patient has had her male, she should be allowed to rest before the next one.

The patient must be told to void any foodstuffs which bring on his symptoms.

A good nourishing duet is also important to keep skin and tissues in good shape.

Do not spoil the patient's nightware by dripping food on it.

You should not try to push the patient with large amounts of food.

The nurse must paws before she inserts the next mouthful into the patient.

The nurse should use all her natural wiles to tempt the patient to cooperate with her, particularly at meal-times.

Sugar is essential if fits are to be used in the body.

Vivacious eating is thought to predispose to peptic ulceration.

The patient was given an alight diet.

Patient's with a tendency to gut should be advised to avoid articles of food rich in purines.

The patient should avoid all matey foods and stick to milk.

Dried fruits such as raisins also fags, should be avoided.

The patient could have some battered toast for his early morning breakfast.

The nurse should note whether the patient's ribs are sticking through her nightdress, if so she is emancipated.

The patient's pate should not be overloaded with food.

If the child does not have sufficient vitamin D, he will grow up with a tendency to rackets.

Sister told the patient that as a special treat she would give him a nicely cooked stake for his lunch.

If a hot male is sent up to the ward quick service will prevent cooling.

He will be given a suit and nourishing diet during his stay in hospital.

The patient is given straw along with his drink.

Proteins are responsible for replacing the wear and tar of tissues.

The patient must be encouraged to drink plenty of coal fluids to help lower the temperature.

The patient should have a feeding cap to help him with fluids.

The doctor always orders the type of individual food for the patient, but it is the nurse's duty to see that the docter's orders are eaten.

The patient did not look well, and said she felt offal.

The patient should have easy excess to the food on his locker.

Danger, Nurse at Work

The buttocks must be brought in line with the hedge on the bed.

Covered bowels on the trolley top will contain all the necessary ingredients to cover the wound.

Mr. Smith can sit belt upright for his lumbar-puncture.

The doctor carefully marks the area which is going to be punched, this is between the 4th and 15th lumbar vertebrae.

The doctor worms his way through the vertebrae until he reaches the intrathecal space.

The patient is pulled to the edge of the bed and his spine is then drawn to get it in position.

The patient is admitted into a well wormed bed.

Special core was given to the patient's pressure areas to harden the skin.

The patient's hare was long and carried germs all over the ward.

The patient's bad linen must never brush the floor.

The nurse must scrub her hinds before she goes near the patient.

The nurse will use an orange stuck with cotton wool to insert into the patient's nostrils for cleaning purposes.

Edward Tudor's spectacles are used for giving oxygen to the patient.

The nurse should wash the fete twice daily.

If the hair is arranged in tidy plants, it will do much to improve the patient's appearance.

The patient's hands must be moved so that the muscles do not loose their power.

If the patient's head is examined and found to be nutty, the nurse can use vinegar to loosen and cure the trouble.

The patient if he is able to understand is then told what is going to happen to him, if he does not understand then it does not matter what the nurse does to him.

It is essential that the patient's fingers and toes should be kept tidy and in place.

A dirty nurse will help the sterile nurse to do the dressings, but she is not allowed near the patient or she may act as a vendor of infection.

Soiled dressings are placed in buns, these are then handed out to the porters.

The patient's fingers should be trimmed to shape before her blanket bath.

Sandbags could be used to prevent the patient's feet from becoming draped.

Nurses should not cling to the sheets when making a patient's bed, as this gives the germs an opportunity to crawl on her apron.

A ring will prevent the patiens getting sores on her soul.

The cublicles on the patient's nails should be pushed down gently.

The patient is washed all over with warm soupy water.

When taking the patient's pulse the nurse should note the number of beaks and record them on the chart.

The patient should first be looked over for signs of defamities.

Female patients can see their hands, male patients do not bother, therefore a perfumed hand lotion will help.

The nurse did not like the dirty jab she was given by sister in the sluice.

The nurse should always wear her musk whilst attending to the patients.

The hands of a patient should always be washed after the use of a bed pin.

If the nurse is wise, she will never let a patient take advantage of her, matron will not help her if this happens.

Shock can be foetal so care must be taken of the patient whilst she is in this condition.

The patient should be encouraged to move his hands all over the bed to prevent hand drop.

If a phony was handy I would get in touch with the surgeon at once.

The nurse must make sure her mast is satisfactory before she ventures to do the patient's dressing.

Usually the patients who come into hospital are not used to lying in bed all the time, and if they are made to, their morality drops and this does not aid the patient's recovery.

On taking the patient's pulse, nurse found it to be string.

When the nurse puts the gown on, it should be inside out and when she hangs it up afterwards it should be outside in.

The bedpan is mapped after use.

The patient will probably have disposable tishoos.

The heels are a potential sight for pressure sores.

The nurse is responsible for the filing of hot water bottles and she should repeat this performance every 4 hours.

If a child is in a steam tent, it is not right that he should be left.

If the patient's heels are read, the nurse will probably see a warning re bedsores.

When moving Mrs Smith, nurse should grasp the other nurses arm and carry it to the foot of the bed.

The best sight for an intramuscular injection is undoubtedly the buttocks.

The sterile pick is placed on the top shelf of the trolley ready for use on the patient's wound.

The trolley tap must be washed with soap and water before anything else is done.

The patient may complain of being sour if he lies in one position for too long.

The child had a look like pane on her face.

Look at the patient carefully when he is admitted to make sure there are no scares present.

The patients may be kept awake by just one nosy patient on the ward.

The patient should have something to do or he will become board.

Every effort should be made to prevent the patient from obtaining bedsores.

After staff nurse has signed for the drugs she must be sure to lick them away carefully.

The treatment consists of robbing the patient's areas with the hands.

The patient may complain of not having any energen, and therefore a very long period of convalescence is required.

The breathing could be sighing due to hare hunger.

The patient was kept in bud until improvement was noted.

The doctor inserted a needle into the spain to draw off C.S.F.

The best position for lumbar puncture is to have the patient curled up like a bull.

The best position to nurse the hemiplegic patient is in the semi prawn position.

A heal pad is placed under the leg to aid its recovery.

The whole of the lag is to be shaved before the procedure.

After wishing, the feet should be carefully dried.

A bed cradle is used to take the weight of the bedclothes off the patient's upper lugs.

Mental crystals can be added to the inhaler as an inducement.

The patient was a little bugger compared with his size a year previously.

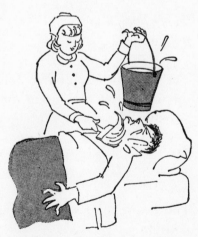

A pint brush may be used for applying lotion to the throat.

The patient should put her head over the jug, take deep breaths and inhale it.

The patient should have a sputum pit by his bedside and he will usually fill this during postural drainage.

The patient who has diarrhoea should be barricade nursed.

If the patient is kept in bed too long he will not circulate well, and thrombosis could be his lot.

A cork bunk is placed in the inhaler before the patient has it.

The patient should hail through the mouth and out through the nose if the inhalation is to be effective.

The patient was unable to go to the toilet, so the nurse sat her upon the bed pin, but the patient did not cooperate very well.

Mrs. Smith's mouth to let has to be dealt with as soon as her visitors had departed.

The heart failer should be nursed in an upright position.

The hair would be tiddly braided by the nurse.

I would keep up his morale by having him shaved by the hospital barker.

If contact is made with such a parson, a full bath to which a disinfectant has been added should be taken as soon as possible.

Watch that the patient does not become a little tyre when she is got up for the first time.

To prevent infection hair should be kept off colour and away from the face.

The patient was given oxygen using naval tubes which were passed along the base.

The patient complained of chipped arms and hands, and was given a hand cream to improve matters.

It was decided that an ice bog might relieve the patient's headache and fever.

The needle should be driven into the tissues by an angel of about 45 for a subcutaneous injection.

The temperature was high and the patient's face was flashing.

The patient was hot and flushed and kept complaining of first.

A builder is placed over the patient's stump to stop it from jumping about the bed.

The nurse should stand behind the patient and irritate the eye from within outwards.

A light male is given at 6 p.m. and then nothing by mouth until after the test.

The nurse must keep her nails closely paired and her skin should not become sore and crocked.

Occupational therapy is given to keep the patient hoppy and contented.

In the knee chest position the patient rusts on knees, arms, and chest.

A fomentation is a method of applying mist heat and is as a rule applied 4 hourly.

Mrs. Church's licker should be within easy reach of her without her having to reach for it.

The patient is told to ring her bell for the nurse if she fancies a drunk.

The nurses would then lift Mr. Smith down the bed using the Australian lift, being careful to make sure his feet were not hanging off over the edge of the bed.

The clean sheets would then be rolled under the patient and tacked in all around the bed.

The nurse should notice whether Mrs. Brown developed a rush after having the medicine.

The wait of the patient should be recorded on entering the hospital, and then at intervals.

The patient may be nursed on a rippling mattress to prevent sores forming.

I would observe whether he was swearing, hot or cold, and then decide whether to tepid sponge or not.

The nurse should do the pressure areas thoroughly, and make sure the annual region is kept clean and free from soreness.

A specimen of urine is obtained for ward tasting.

The patient should never be led down in the bed if he is breathless.

The bed is neatly stripped and the patient covered with a worm blanket.

A good nurse is a curtain nurse when dealing with drugs, otherwise she is a menass.

The nurse should not treat her elderly patient's like simpletons. They are always much more intelligent than the nurses looking after them these days.

The patient should always have a ball so that she can attract the nurse's attention when she wants anything.

The pain killing drug which has been made up in liquid foam can be given by mouth or by injection.

Mrs. Jones bed would be clanged from top to bottom to make her feel fresh and comfortable.

The pressure areas must be dyed and powdered frequently to prevent sores forming.

Mr. Smith must be nursed with great care because of his falling heart.

The patient must always be in a position which places least stain on the heart.

The student nurse must always report to the train nurse or her sister when going on and off duty.

The patient should be told to adopt a laxative position when sitting on the bedpan.

The nurse must also observe the position of the patient's limbs, and make sure that no listing deformities result from her neglect.

The patient was nursed in Fowler's position, but would keep slapping down the bed.

The cradle was placed over the patient's legs to prevent foot drip.

Patients must be encouraged to drink plenty of coal fluids to help lower the temperature.

The patient should be nursed in the semi cucumbent position for best results.

A buck rest is useful to keep the patient upright.

The patient should be able to open her drawers without placing strain on her heart.

The top of the file is removed and the rest of it is then injected into the patient making sure he gets it all.

If the patient is obese, the nurse should certainly put her eye on him.

All this patient's fluids should be placed on a fluid cart together with all her urine and faeces.

All many patients want to do on admission to hospital is to be a liar in bed all day.

After attending to the patient, the nurse goes to the ball and washes her hands.

The nurse should use every measure she can think of to promote bed sores in her patients.

The patient's weight should be recorded at the entrance to ths hospital and weekly thereafter.

Any linen with tares in it should be taken out of circulation.

The rubber tubing from the oxygen cylinder goes to a wolf.

The nurse takes the soiled sheets from the bed and places them in the linen ship.

The bed is made on the top part of the patient first and then the nurses work round to his bottom.

If the patient breathes through his mouth he will be perched.

If the patient is nursed flat, be careful he does not swallow his tong.

The patient's bet is made each morning with two nurses.

The patient should be nursed on a nipple mattress.

The patient should have a sputum carton on his locker, because he is always expecting sputum.

The patient will do better if he is nursed in a three quarter prune position.

The patient was fat, and this was obviously due to ademon.

All the pillows not actually required should be placed on a char at the side of the bed.

The patient is lifted down the bed by an Australian if she is breathless.

After the enema a pun should be offered to the patient.

All the soiled linen from the bed should be placed in billy carrier.

The patient should be treated as a hole and not just her ulcer.

If the adult in hospital is a child, he may miss his parents.

Not only does the patient's physical condition deteriorate, but also their spiritual condition. They become very depressed and are aggressive and very often crawl in a little shell from which they often do not emerge from for days, and this retards their physical condition.

Nurse remembering her lectures on nurse/patient relationship and tried beyond endurance by a particularly difficult patient, lost her control at last and flung at him "Oh you, you, human being".

When a patient has been in the ward for a long time, it is to be expected that the nurses will be happily related to him.

The patient should be given national health service treatment except when he is in a private room.

Cleanliness is Next to Godliness

If the patient is found to be suffering from poison an anecdote should be found as soon as possible.

The patient was lifted and transfixed to the ambulance.

If the patient is bleeding from the leg, press your thumb firmly in her groan.

If Johny has swallowed tablets, first aid treatment is to make him sick and give them back.

The methods of respiration which would be used are mouth to moth, and an alternative is trafalgar nelson's method.

Mouth to mouth breathing—You then remove your mouth from the patient's and allow her to expire gently away.

Silver vests method will often restore the patient's breathing to normal.

If the patient breaks a leg, it should be strapped with the other to keep it still.

If cardiac arrest is to be treated a large bard is placed in the patient's bed.

A first aider should do fast things first.

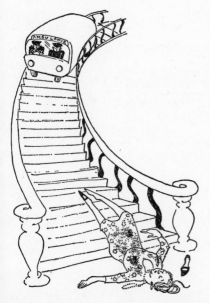

If a tourniquet is applied to this patient, you must not forget to place a tee on his head.

The mouth to mouth breathing tube goes down to the anal pharynx.

A clover hitch sling was used to rest the patient's arm.

On finding an elderly patient unconscious at the foot of the stairs, an ambulance should be brought to that spot to remove her.

Comprehensive haemorrhage may occur after several days due to sepsis.

I would cut the patient's trousers up the seamy side in order to gain access to the required area.

Flies may not be easy to catch, but food should never be left uncovered in the kitchen. The fly may have just come from sitting on a bedpan to perch on the uncovered food.

The nurses appeared to enjoy their lectures on public health from the heath visitor.

Flies are dangerous and should be dealt with by drastic means if seen flying around the ward.

The patient would be resettled in a satiable occupation with the cooperation of the almoner.

The patient said he had been troubled by flees.

The patient's hijeans must be dealt with regularly.

The adult worm produces lather in the host's tissues.

Bed spacing is arranged so that each patient has 1200 feet.

The new Minister of Health is a man whose political beliefs may affect the health of his parishioners.

Enemas are given to clean out the bowels. This is a soup and water enema. Another type is nutritional; giuen by a drip.

A good nurse never sweats. It is essential that she uses an antiperspirant which will paralyse all her follicles.

The freshness of the nurse determines the patients morals.

The nurses chapel is frequently used for matings in the evenings.

Is He Bad, Doctor?

Straining the stool of a patient suffering from ulcerative colitis will cause perforation of the bowl.

Constipation may be presented and the patient will often complain bitterly if it is.

The patient was admitted to a medical ward in a state of confusion.

The patient complained of the pain which was radiator down the arm.

The patient was suffering from a white cell condition called lookocytoesis.

The doctor pointed out that his patient Mrs. Church, was an interesting cuss, and the post grads should examinine her.

The patient should be told to avoid rushing around taking things easy.

A patch of herpes often breaks out on the patient's laps.

The patient was obviously suffering from heart failure because her ankles were balloons.

The patient may develop hydrostatic pneumonia.

If in trouble I would send for medical acid to fix the patient.

The onset of lober pneumonia is usually sodden.

The pulse beat may be observed in the temple.

The doctor thought that the hate regulating centre in the brain was responsible for his troubles.

A power lass will be seen if the patient does not activate himself in his bed.

One less common type of anaemia seen these day is known as pernickity anaemia.

As the patient was suffering from jaund-ice, the sister gave instructions that if the butler was used a small portion was quite enough.

The anaemic patient should have a mallow puncture, and this should be done through his stern.

If the patient is suffer-ing from wheel's disease he will most certainly be yellow.

When Mrs. Patey who has been suffering from a heart condition is discharged she should be told to live below ground level.

A woman's pulse is generally much quacker than a man's.

A further complication may be due to rapture on part of the ulcer.

The patient should be warned he is radio activated.

The condition is extremely common in muddle aged women.

Pyelitis occurs more readily in women than men, because the germs have fewer obstacles to surmount on their way to the urinary track.

The ataxia of tables is very much worse after a period of confinement to bed.

In general paralysis of the insane, the patient develops coarse tremors of the lips and hands, and argyll highlanders pupils.

Bazaar conduct is often associated with hallucinated and deluded patients.

The temperature of the body is the balance between hate produced and hate lost.

Cases of the mildest forms of mental deficiency are termed feeble minded, or mormons.

The woman was investigated and the physician diagnosed the case as one of Bill's Palsy.

Some patients are given gold, this pleases them and their arthritis is often seen to improve.

The doctor after examining Mr. Brown said he was a sack nan and needed admitting urgently.

Sunny is the mildest form of dysentery found in this country.

The patient was admitted for investigation, the fits she had been having regularly were thought to be historical and not epileptic.

The patient's blood should be typed and criss cross matched.

The patient often complained of musty vision.

The doctor just walked on to the ward at 11 p.m. to do his nightie round.

Thread worms are like small pieces of cotton when seen in the thesis in the bedpan.

The patient's tongue was covered with furs.

Below the Belt

It is important to make sure the patient washes herself and dries the uterus carefully after using the bedpan.

Nurse said she would have to do her midwiffing after she had finished her general training.

An inevitable abortion is when the mother has given up hope.

A nurse's work is of great impotence.

When the male patient was asked why he wished to purchase tampax for himself he replied, "I have been told that users of tampax can swim, dance, ride a bicycle etc., and I can do none of these things."

If these tests are normal a carved sort of sound is often passed to her bladder.

The surgeon said he would examine the patient's bladder with the help of Sister scope.

Women, shortly after the men pause, sometimes develop hot blushes.

The woman was diagnosed as suffering from snail vaginitis common in the elderly.

Mrs. Brown was worried about her genial prolapse, but the surgeon assured her he would fix it.

After a repair operation the patient should be told not to be bothered with married life after she leaves the hospital.

The patient's genitals were swapped before the treatment began.

A special virginal pessary was ordered for Miss Brown.

After the douche the residual fluid may be removed by pressure on the patient's pubs.

These pessaries cause the vagina to discharge excess fluid particularly rubber.

The uterus may be prevented from popping out by indicating the need for a watch spring.

The patient is placed in Sam's semiprone position to have the pessary inserted.

A penile hood was placed over the patient before he was catheterised.

The patient was passing wine frequently, because he said his bladder irritated him.

If the incontinent patient is a male, a Paul's tub can be placed over his penis to keep him dry.

If the patient can't sleep it may be because he cannot empty his bladder, or wants to go to the toilet, in the latter case give it to him.

The patient complained that his tastes were swollen, and a scrotal support would help to improve them.

If the patient is a male, it would be best to strap his penis with a tube like strap, Paul's will do. He will then perhaps keep his bed dry.

A penile clap is necessary before the local anaesthetic is introduced in to his urethra.

The underlying principle of this test is that if a patient is kept without water he should pass concencrated urine.

The nurse pulls the prepuce back with her gaze, and then discards it into a receiver.

The patient was asked to pass the urine specimen whilst lying in bed, into a specimen glass which the nurse has placed on the trolley at the foot of the bed.

Before the patient is asked for a mid stream specimen of water, his glands must be swabbed all over with an antiseptic.

The catheter is inserted via the urethral office into the bladder.

The urinal should be put in a private place, and the patient will then see what he can do.

Bones, Germs and Drugs

The patient's ear sacks may become dilated resulting in emphysema.

The patient's longs were not good therefore he was short in breathing.

The stern one is situated in front of the patient's chest and keeps his ribs apart.

The faecal bones number 14, those forming the cheek being most prominent.

The proper name for the heel bone is the os selsey.

The capsule which surrounds the liver is known as a glistener.

The intricate factor secreted by the stomach sometimes fails hence anaemia strikes the patient making him yellow all over.

The pulse rate is usually 60-80 beats per minute in adults, slightly more in women.

The bronchi are supplied by a vague nerve.

A man is a backboned human animal.

The heart is like a muscular pimp, serving the body in which it is placed.

A sensible neurone conveys impulses from the outside world to the brain.

A long bone of the limbs consists of a central park, the shaft, and two ends.

The blood plates are responsible for the control of blood escaping from its vessels, they act by blocking the exits.

The blood consists of a fluid with bodies floating in it.

The spinal cord gives off nerves which are seen as pears.

The membranes of the alimentary tract secrete muckus.

Blood may cause bad reactions if it does not belong to a negative rhesus monkey.

Each kidney contains many bowmen, each having a job to do.

When we touch something hot with our fingers we draw our four arms away.

Micturition is under the control of the higher centres which can keep the sphinster contracted.

Dressings are best done by the nun touch technique.

There are large men brains all over the body inside e.g. lining the guts.

The pulse is a wave of dissension passing along the artery wall.

A cross infection committee was set up in the hospital to deal with affection between nurses and patients.

The patient's blood pleasure may be raised.

To sterilise a rubber catheter, you should run under a tap letting the water go in your top and out your bottom. When this has been done a few times bottom up should be the order so that the water can come out the top. After all this, boil for 5 minutes and sterility should be certain.

A means of spread is by the droplet method, masks are worn to catch them before they fall on the patient's face.

Floor cleaning is best done with a hover type machine to prevent cross infection.

Man, like birds and other mammals is a warm bloody animal.

The disease is caused by an organism called Nasser's gonorrhoea.

Disease is nearly always caused by gems. Nurses carry many of these.

The patient's liver should be kept separate if he is infectious.

Extra heat would be needed to kill the sporting type of bacteria.

One of the most common types of food poisoning is that caused by an organism known as the salmon.

If a patient is infectious some crocks are put in the cell with her and no one else will touch them again.

If anyone is seen carrying typhoid around, that person should be removed from society and made clean.

Cross infection is always blamed on nurses, but the real bugbearers in this respect are the docters who think they are too pure to carry such things as germs.

The dressings should first have been autoclawed.

If more than one case of an infectious disease is reported in a district the M.O.H. will think an epidemic is about to break and will order the Town Hall to work on Saturday mornings to stamp it out.

The organisms may be transported by an air carrier thus infecting many unsuspecting people.

You should rinse in cold water first to remove the stairs, and then boil for 5 minutes.

The organisms by an inspiration enter the body and do their deadly deeds.

Germs bread in stiffy conditions.

The ward drugs should be kept in a coal dark place.

Phenobarbitone may be given to seduce the patient and put his mind at rest.

The patient was given dregs to treat his condition with good effect.

The patient was given a string purgative to overcome his constipation.

Welldone tablets were given to put the patient to sleep for the night.

Ergometrine is given to control the behaviour of the woman's uterus.

The B.P. is a list of officious drugs which have proved their usefulness.

D.D. drugs must be chucked by a state registered nurse before they can be given to a patient.

Care of the moth is important and atropine may be given to dry up its secretions.

Nystatin is prepared as virginal pessaries, each containing 100,000 units of the drug.

Drugs should have the correct amount in the box at the start so that anybody can take any out without nobody knowing.

If the patient did not like the taste of his medicine, give him a sweat to go with the next dose.

All prisons must be kept locked up in the proper cupboard.

Make sure the bottle to be used is well corkered.

The drug may be sprayed into the patient's tracker.

Drugs of abdication are kept in a special locked cupboard in the ward.

The patient was given an expectorant for his coffin.

Atropine is given to quieten the patient's mouth during the operation.

Martha is used by some thoracic surgeons to sedate the patient instead of morphia the former stimulates and does not make the patient dopy.

When a drug has been prescribed for a patient, the nurse along with another nurse must chuck several things.

The patient was given a dose of cocane, this being applied to his skin.

The nurse would pour the drug into a medicine glass holding the cork in her little finger and making sure the labia was uppermost.

The patient was given the drug and a swallow after it.

Whilst pouring the dose of medicine the nurse should hold the conk in her little finger.

About a ½ hour after giving the drug, the nurse should ask the patient if the pain has subsisted.

Xylocaine jelly can be used in a strength of 2% when dealing with certain mail procedures.

The patient was given a dose of chloral hydrant whenever it was required.

The pain killing drug is written up by the doctor who has seen Mrs. Elvin on a drug chart.

If the patient's chat is in order, the sedative should be given.

Just Skin and Bones

The patient was admitted with a rodent on his face, care of the skin specialist.

A popular rash may occur where the rosealar rash was situated.

The papules on the patient were dame shaped and were therefore hard when touched.

Scabies is characterised by a hitchy paperlar rash on the wrists and other areas.

Blackheads can be removed by gentle pressure with an instrument called a comedian extractor.

Acne rosary is a skin disease affecting certain women.

The patient was seen by the shin specialist who ordered her face to be covered with cream.

Papules are small solid spits.

A very strong back slap was the treatment for the broken shin bone.

Vesicles are small blusterers.

The broken leg can be tied to the other lamb, this will keep both still.

The patient broke his collar bone and caused his arm to drip.

The woman said she had been sent to the Out Patient's department because she had a bunny on her big toe.

A compound fracture is one where the tissues are broken and air rushes in to take their place. This results in bacteria following and settling down to breed.

The physiotherapist visits the wards every day to give a message to the patient's limbs.

If the patient has a fractured skill he should be nursed with one pillow for 24 hours.

Sin traction is done to overcome the pulling bones.

The physiotherapist will have to excise all the patient's muscles before his operation to give him a chance to survive.

Mr. Jones was now at the stage when he should be measured for clutches.

The patient is placed in a fracture bed so that he can heel.

By the position of the externally rotated foot it was obviously a broken female neck.

The patient was able to travel around the ward in spite of her fracture, by means of tripots.

The fractured leg is propped three times before the patient goes to theatre. This should be done very carefully.

Incisive Surgery

Mr. Smith has had an abominable perineal excision of her rectum.

The patient on being brought back from the operating theatre, was placed in a corner on top of the ward.

The patient was alarmed when he heard the surgeon tell his houseman to watch for gastric bash.

The young woman told the house surgeon she had a definite limp in her breast and that she noticed it every time she got in the bath.

Ward Report: Fairly good day. 20 fl. oz. of drainage from the intercoastal tube.

The patient was admitted with an injury to his hod. This was sutured and the patient was admitted.

An infernal haemorrhage was diagnosed.

The surgeon decided that a Russell Venom traction was the best form of treatment for the leg.

The patient was stupidose after the knock on his head.

A ship is sent to the matron's office to give her the news of the patient's operation.

The surgeon was told to expect presents of sepsis in his ward.

The patient had had an operation for the removal of his tinsels.

Nurse should make sure the patient's belly button is free from grease before she sends her off.

The male surgical ward sister said she thought the ward was stuffy, and directed nurse to see to the widows to improve matters.

In advanced cases a hard miss can be felt in the patient's abdomen.

The proctoscope is a short tub designed for examination of the rectum.

The child should be given a general's anaesthetic.

Patient's with complete obstruction of the common bile duct, become more and more deeply jaundiced and may eventually look like an olive.

The "T" tube was in the patient to make sure his boil got away.

A peptic ulcer may explode through the muscular will of the stomach.

The patient should have nail by mouth for 12 hours before the operation.

The patient must be given a clean cop before she is sent to the theatre.

The patient's teeth are removed, but it is the duty of the nurse to put them all back when he has recovered from his anaesthetic.

Anything false about the patient should be remedied before he is allowed to go for his operation.

Before the female patient goes to the theatre her hair is enclosed in a triangle to keep it away from the surgeon.

The theatre sister said the nurses would be coloured green when they entered theatre.

All the patients records including his urine are chucked before going to the operating theatre.

The surgeon will operate in a field which has been gone over carefully by the nurses.

See that the patient is shaved from the nipper line to the thighs.

In order that the patient is not mislaid, he is labelled on his wrist before going for his operation.

A female patient's head may be covered by a squire this will conceal her hair.

Mr. Jones should be encouraged to walk up and over the ward to get the use back in his mussels.

In an emergency the patient's vane is opened and some of the contents allowed to escape into a receiver.

It is best that the patient should have a thorough bath before his operation, as he may not need another afterwards.

The surgeon's horseman hastened around the ward.

A specimen bottle was required by the houseman as he wished to deposit the patient's blood he had just eliminated.

Nurse told matron her stays in theatre for the whole 2 month period proved to be uncomfortable for her.

In intravenous anaesthesia suitable gents are injected straight into the patient's bloodstream.

The patient was continually complaining of hearth burn after he had taken his meals.

If the female patient is made up, the nurse should remove the make up so that the anaesthetist can see when she is dying in the theatre.

Oddments

Smoking with an empty stomach should be avoided.

Lament from student nurses which was refused by the hospital magazine:

> Old nurses never die,
> They do not fade away,
> They have no interests to indulge,
> So, we see them every day.
>
> They get on all committees,
> They're examiners for evermore,
> They seek to run our lives for us,
> By what has gone before.
>
> Oh! would that some kind body could,
> A course for them devise,
> To prepare them for the outside world,
> When retirement day arrives.

3